HARRIET
TUBMAN

and the
Underground Railroad

by Dan Elish

GATEWAY CIVIL RIGHTS
THE MILLBROOK PRESS
BROOKFIELD, CONNECTICUT

Photographs courtesy of: the Cincinnati Art Museum ("The Underground Railroad" by Charles T. Webber): cover; Culver Pictures: cover inset, p. 11; Library of Congress: pp. 1, 7, 8, 18, 25, 27; Sophia Smith Collection, Smith College: pp. 2–3; UPI/Bettmann Newsphotos: pp. 4, 12, 14, 26; The Metropolitan Art Museum: p. 16; The Schomburg Center: pp. 21, 29; The Brooklyn Museum: p. 22; Harriet Tubman Home, Auburn, N.Y.: p. 30.

Library of Congress Cataloging-in-Publication Data

Elish, Dan.
Harriet Tubman and the underground railroad /
by Dan Elish.
    p.   cm.—(Gateway civil rights)
Includes bibliographical references and index.
Summary: A biography of the African American woman who escaped from slavery, led slaves to freedom on the Underground Railroad, aided Northern troops during the Civil War, and worked for women's suffrage.
ISBN 1-56294-273-5 (lib. bdg.)
    1. Tubman, Harriet, 1820?–1913—Juvenile literature.   2. Slaves—United States—Biography—Juvenile literature.   3. Afro-Americans—Biography—Juvenile literature.   4. Underground railroad—Juvenile literature. [1. Tubman, Harriet, 1820?–1913.   2. Slaves.   3. Afro-Americans—Biography.   4. Underground railroad.]   I. Title.
II. Series.
E444.T82E45   1993
305.5'67'092—dc20
[B]   92-9562   CIP   AC

Published by The Millbrook Press
2 Old New Milford Road
Brookfield, Connecticut 06804

Harriet Tubman poses with runaways whom she has led safely out of slavery.

Eleven slaves had been on the run for days. Very tired and weak from hunger, they stopped to rest in the woods. One large man said that he could not go on. He was heading back south to the plantation. But he fell silent at the touch of cold steel on the back of his neck.

"Move or die!" said a low, harsh voice.

A sturdy woman half the man's size held the pistol. She had a deep scar above her left eyebrow. Her name was Harriet Tubman, and she meant what she said.

The man sighed and pushed himself up onto his feet. Then the group walked slowly off again into the inky night, heading north to freedom.

At that time, several years before the beginning of the Civil War, millions of black Americans were enslaved in the South. They often worked under very harsh conditions. The only release was escape, but few found the courage.

By the time Abraham Lincoln became president in 1860, Harriet Tubman had made the journey north some nineteen times. She led as many as three hundred slaves to freedom. Each trip was very dangerous, but Tubman was never caught.

She kept her troops moving a step ahead of the slave catchers and trained dogs that were sure to be on their trail. She did not let anyone turn back for fear that they would be beaten and forced to tell where the other slaves had gone.

Harriet Tubman used to sing in a low, quiet voice as the group marched along. The others would join in, and their spirits would rise. One of her favorite songs was about Moses, the biblical figure who led the Jews out of slavery in Egypt.

Go down, Moses,
Way down in Egyptland,
Tell old Pharaoh,
To let my people go.

To blacks and whites who were against slavery, Harriet Tubman was known as Moses. She led more people out of slavery in the South into the Promised Land of the North than any other person in history.

Born into Misery

Harriet Tubman was born into slavery around 1820. Her name was Araminta Ross, but she was called Harriet after her mother. The exact date of her birth is unknown. Because few slaves could read or write, such records were rare.

Harriet grew up in a small cabin in the slave quarters of a large plantation in Dorchester County, Maryland. She lived with her father, Benjamin Ross (known as Old Ben), her mother,

Harriet Green (known as Old Rit), and her ten sisters and brothers. Her grandparents were both West Africans who had been captured by slave traders and brought to America in chains.

Harriet's earliest memory was of other slaves who lived in the quarters sneaking to her parents' cabin at night. They came to talk, mostly about how they longed to be free. Even more, they hated living with the constant threat of being sold and separated from their families.

Slaves lived crowded together in run-down shacks.

Then, one day when Harriet was five years old, the Ross family's owner, Edward Brodas, sold two of her sisters "down south." The life of a slave on a cotton plantation in the Deep South states was often much more harsh than in the states of Maryland, Kentucky, and Virginia. To be sold south was seen as a fate as terrible as death.

After her sisters were sold, Harriet prayed every night that she would never be taken from her parents. But that same year, Brodas "rented" her to the Cooks, a poor white couple who couldn't afford to own a slave outright. Miserable, Harriet was torn from her home.

The Cooks lived in a small, ill-kept cabin. Harriet slept on the floor in the kitchen near the fireplace and shared scraps of food with the dogs. Mrs. Cook, a weaver, made Harriet spend endless hours in a dusty, dark room making cloth. Harriet hated the work, but whenever she complained, she was severely scolded. And Mr. Cook forced the little girl, dressed only in a thin shirt, to wade daily in the shallows of an ice-cold river checking his muskrat traps. Harriet became very sick. The Cooks sent her back to the Brodas plantation only when she was close to death.

There, her mother nursed her slowly back to health. But as soon as Harriet recovered, she was rented out again, this time to a large plantation house. Her new mistress, Miss Susan, was even crueler than the Cooks had been. Within only a few days, Harriet had marks all over her neck and back from Miss Susan's whip.

Harriet wanted to run back to her mother, but she was scared, and she didn't know the way. Then one morning Miss Susan caught her taking a cube of

A white woman whips a black girl, just as Harriet was whipped by Miss Susan.

sugar from the breakfast table. "The next minute she had the rawhide down," Harriet recalled years later. "I give one jump out of the door and I saw that they came after me, but I just flew and they didn't catch me."

Harriet ran as far as she could before collapsing in a pigpen. She hid there for four days, fighting the pigs for scraps of slop. In the end, she was so starved that she returned to Miss Susan. After a sound whipping, Miss Susan sent Harriet back to her parents, saying she wasn't "worth a sixpence."

Scarred for Life

Despite these hardships, Minta, as Harriet was called by her family, grew up to be a strong worker. By age eleven, she was sweating in the fields, a bright bandanna tied around her head.

Still, Harriet dreamed of freedom. Names of slaves who had run away were whispered around the slave quarters. One man, Tice Davids, swam across the Ohio River from Kentucky.

Harriet overheard his owner say: "He must have gone on an underground railroad."

She was puzzled. Was there some sort of magical railroad that brought people north to freedom?

It wasn't until she was thirteen that Harriet herself witnessed an escape. It was fall corn-harvest time. Harriet and the rest of the slaves sang loudly, husking corn to the driving rhythm. As the sun was sinking below the rim of the hill, a slave took off as fast as he could across the field. The overseer, the man hired by the owner to make sure that the slaves worked hard, grabbed his whip and was after him like a shot. Harriet couldn't help herself. She ran after the overseer to see what would happen next.

The runaway ducked into a store and was cornered inside. The overseer ordered Harriet to hold the slave so that he could whip him. But she stood in the doorway, frozen with fear. When the slave bolted for the door, the overseer picked up a heavy lead weight from the counter and threw it at the fleeing man. The weight struck Harriet instead, knocking her out cold.

Harriet lay in a coma for weeks and was bedridden until the following spring. No one knew exactly what was wrong with her, but she had probably suffered a fractured skull and a severe concussion. Once again, Old Rit nursed her daughter back to health. But this time Harriet carried a scar that was even more serious than those she had gotten from Miss Susan.

From that time on, she would suffer from terrible headaches, and she would suddenly fall into a deep sleep several

A runaway heads for a swamp with white men on horseback hot on his heels.

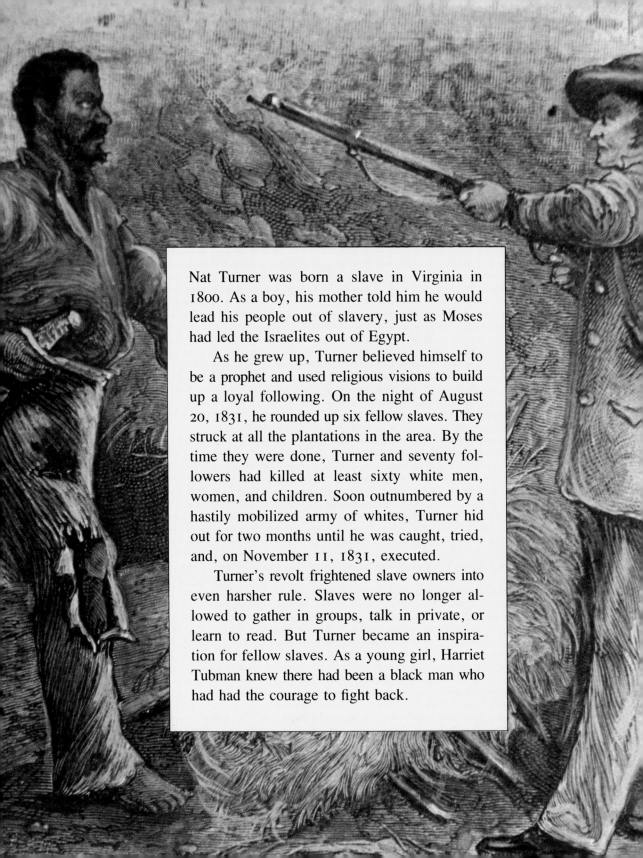

Nat Turner was born a slave in Virginia in 1800. As a boy, his mother told him he would lead his people out of slavery, just as Moses had led the Israelites out of Egypt.

As he grew up, Turner believed himself to be a prophet and used religious visions to build up a loyal following. On the night of August 20, 1831, he rounded up six fellow slaves. They struck at all the plantations in the area. By the time they were done, Turner and seventy followers had killed at least sixty white men, women, and children. Soon outnumbered by a hastily mobilized army of whites, Turner hid out for two months until he was caught, tried, and, on November 11, 1831, executed.

Turner's revolt frightened slave owners into even harsher rule. Slaves were no longer allowed to gather in groups, talk in private, or learn to read. But Turner became an inspiration for fellow slaves. As a young girl, Harriet Tubman knew there had been a black man who had had the courage to fight back.

times a day. These blackouts would be dangerous for both Moses and her followers as they fled the slave catchers on their way to a new land.

Hired Out

Harriet was not fully healed when she learned that she was to be sold down south. Brodas did not want to keep such a troublesome slave around. Harriet prayed with all her might not to be taken from her family again. She even prayed that Brodas would die. Then she was shocked to hear that Brodas had in fact died. Harriet felt very guilty. She thought that her prayers had caused his death.

A clergyman named Anthony Thompson was put in charge of the plantation until Brodas's son would become old enough to run it himself. As soon as Harriet was able to work again, Thompson hired her out with her father to a builder named John Stewart. Harriet asked him if she could work outside with the men, chopping down trees and splitting logs. Stewart agreed.

Harriet loved being outdoors. Even more, she loved working with her father. Ben taught her everything he knew about nature: which berries were safe to eat, how to study the position of the stars at night, how to walk silently through the woods. Although they never talked about it, Harriet knew that her father was preparing her for the day when she would run away.

Toward the end of this period, Harriet met John Tubman, a free black man. In 1844 they were married, and Harriet went to live in his cabin. Now Harriet wanted to be free more than ever. She couldn't stand knowing that at any time she could be sold away from her husband.

Harriet told her husband that she wanted to escape. He only laughed and even warned that he would turn her in if she tried. Harriet was shocked and hurt. But John was happy with his life. He was free and didn't want to make waves with the powerful white men who ruled the state.

First Trip

In the late 1840s, Harriet's worst fears came true. Brodas's son died, and Thompson decided to sell some slaves. Two of Tubman's sisters were put in chains and sold to new owners.

It was not uncommon for a slave mother to be sold and taken away from her children.

Tubman knew that there was no time to lose. She had heard about a white woman who helped runaways. One day the woman was riding in a carriage through the field where she was working, and Tubman dared to speak to her. The woman listened carefully and then said the words that would change Tubman's life: "If you ever need any help, Harriet, why you let me know."

Tubman could not believe her ears. Who would have thought that a white woman would be willing to help her? But she was still frightened. What if the woman was lying? What if her husband turned her in, or she fell asleep along the way and was caught?

But the terror of being sold south was more powerful than her fears. Tubman convinced three of her brothers to go with her. That night they took off. But they didn't know the woods and the night sky like their sister did. They talked, tripped, and jumped at every strange sound.

Finally they stopped and said that they were going to turn back. Harriet argued and even tried to fight them, but she was outnumbered. She had no choice but to go back before her escape was noticed and wait for another chance.

Three days later, Tubman's brothers were in chains on their way south to Georgia. Panicked, Tubman knew she had to act fast and head north alone. Later in life, she explained her decision: "There was one of two things I had *right* to, liberty or death; if I could not have one, I would have the other; for no man should take me alive.''

And so, that night, after her husband was asleep, she tied some corn cakes and salt herring in an old bandanna and set out for points north.

"On to Liberty," by Theodor Kaufmann.

Free
at Last

Harriet Tubman took to the woods and headed straight for Bucktown, to the home of the lady in the wagon. She knocked nervously on the farmhouse door.

"It's Harriet," she whispered.

The woman let her in and wrote down two names and addresses on a small piece of paper. These were Tubman's next safe stopping places. Tubman gave the woman a patchwork quilt she had sewn in thanks and went on her way.

And so, Tubman began her first trip on the Underground Railroad. This was not a railroad in the usual sense. There were no trains, no stations or tracks. This railroad was made instead of a group of people who risked their own safety to help slaves get north to freedom. Some of these people were Quakers, followers of a religion that thought slavery was wrong. These kind people opened their homes to hundreds of slaves. They gave them a place to rest and fed them before they made their way to the next safe stop.

Runaway slaves were advertised on handbills, leaflets that included a picture and a description of the slave. Tubman was quite short and had a huge scar on her forehead. She knew she would be easy to identify.

Reward notices for capture of runaways were nailed to posts and buildings.

She made it to her second stop, however. Another woman took her in, and that night the husband hid her in a wagon of fruits and vegetables and drove through the night. When he stopped, he told Tubman to follow a river and to travel only at night to avoid patrols. It was a tough journey. Along the way, she hid in haystacks and attics. Once, she curled up in a hole where potatoes were kept in the cabin of some free blacks. Finally, thanks to the kindness of many strangers, her own courage, and a little luck, Tubman crossed into Pennsylvania. She was free at last.

"Stranger in a strange land"

Even freedom was difficult, though. "There was no one to welcome me," Tubman later said. "I was a stranger in a strange land, and my home after all was down in the old cabin quarter with the old folks, and my brothers and sisters."

But she made her way to Philadelphia, where she found work as a hotel cook. She also found new friends. The abolitionist movement was made of men and women, white and black, who believed that slavery should be abolished, or ended. Tubman spent many hours with the Philadelphia Vigilance Committee, a group of abolitionists set up to help runaway slaves, or fugitives.

One day, Tubman learned that another sister and her children were about to be sold. The Vigilance Committee knew how to get them to Baltimore, but it needed someone to bring them the rest of the way north. William Still, the Vigilance Committee chairman and a free black man, didn't want Tubman to risk going back for them. But Tubman wouldn't take no for an answer. She was soon off on the first of many trips back into slave territory.

By the time Tubman's sister and her family had made it to Baltimore, their handbill was tacked up everywhere. Fearlessly, Tubman guided them from one stop to the next, bringing them safely to Philadelphia.

The next spring Harriet Tubman went south again and returned with a brother and two other men. During the summer of 1851, Tubman worked in a hotel in Cape May, New Jersey. She saved her money in order to prepare for a special trip down south. This time she was going to bring back her husband, John Tubman.

But when Harriet Tubman reached her old plantation, she was heartbroken to learn that John Tubman had married another woman. She could not convince him to leave his new wife and come north with her. Hurt and angry, Tubman collected a handful of slaves who wanted to be free and took them north instead. This was the first of many groups of strangers she would lead to freedom.

North Against South

Around this time, Northerners and Southerners began to fight bitterly over the issue of slavery. In the North, many people thought that slavery should be abolished throughout the country. But Southerners did not agree. They depended on slave labor to help run their plantations and businesses. As the United States spread west, the North and South argued about which new territories should be free and which should allow slavery.

In 1850, Congress passed a compromise, an act that tried to please both the North and the South. California was admitted as a free state. In return, the North agreed that even when runaway slaves reached the North, they could be hunted down and returned to their owners. This new, harsher ruling was called the Fugitive Slave Act.

Harriet Tubman, known as Moses, became an almost magical figure of great courage.

A slave family gallops toward freedom.

Tubman realized that no ex-slave could be truly safe anywhere in the United States. So, in 1852, she began leading her fugitives all the way to Canada. She came to love that land, where slavery was illegal and where black people had the right to sit on a jury and to vote. For the next six years Harriet Tubman spent winters in the city of St. Catharines, Ontario, and summers in New Jersey working at a hotel. In spring and fall she headed to Maryland to lead more slaves to freedom.

Harriet Tubman's fame grew with each heroic trip. Everyone, even the slave owners, knew about Moses, the great slave runner who could see in the dark, move silently through the thickest forest, and outfight anyone. Owners did what they could to stop her, but they were always a step too late. Most of them thought that Moses was a man. Who else but a man could steal away so many slaves? Many slaveholders believed that Moses was magic.

Riding North

The United States was drawing closer to civil war. The Compromise of 1850 hadn't been enough to ease Southern worries. The North thought slavery was evil; the South didn't like the North meddling in its affairs.

As tempers flared across the country, Tubman quietly kept on with her work. She brought her brothers and sisters-in-law over the Canadian border. Once she led a group of doubtful slaves by gunpoint across an icy river. On another of her trips, while disguised as an old woman, she happened to bump into her former owner Anthony Thompson. Luckily, he didn't realize that the stooped old woman was his ex-slave, Moses herself.

There now remained one trip that Tubman wanted to make more than all others. In 1857 she headed south to bring her parents to freedom. Ben and Rit were elderly, too old to walk. That didn't shake Tubman's confidence, though.

She arrived at the Brodas plantation late at night. She broke into the stable, bridled one of Thompson's horses, and found a rickety old wagon for it to pull. If her parents couldn't make the journey on foot, they'd simply have to ride! She drove them off right through the middle of town in one of her most daring escapades ever. The news traveled fast—Tubman was unstoppable.

She made it with her parents to St. Catharines, but the Canadian winter was too cold for such an old couple. Despite the Fugitive Slave Act, Harriet moved her parents to Auburn, New York, a somewhat safe town with a warmer climate. There, Ben and Rit lived out their lives in freedom.

Speech Maker and Spy

By the years just before the Civil War, Tubman's reputation had spread all across the North. In 1858 she was asked to speak at an anti-slavery rally in Boston. She hesitated at first, but soon threw herself into her speech. She described in detail the difficulties of her many trips along the Underground Railroad. When she was done, the audience leapt to its feet and cheered.

From that day on, she spoke at rallies all across Massachusetts. In a rich, deep voice she talked about the misery of slav-

JOHN BROWN

John Brown was an energetic man who felt that slavery was so wrong that he organized a band of men to start a slave revolt. He wanted Harriet Tubman's help. One day at an abolitionist meeting he spoke to Tubman about his plan. At first she had mixed feelings. She remembered all too well from her childhood days the horrible violence of Nat Turner's revolt. But finally, Brown's firm determination and honesty won Harriet Tubman over, and she gave him her support on his mission.

But John Brown's revolt didn't come off as planned. On October 17, 1859, his uprising ended in disaster when ten of his men were killed. Brown himself was tried, sentenced to death, and hanged on December 2, 1859. Tubman was deeply moved that a white man would care enough to give his life for slaves.

People all over the United States found out about this battle. Some were angry, while those who were against slavery were inspired to fight the system even harder. During the Civil War, Northern soldiers marched into battle singing a song called "John Brown's Body."

ery and the joy of freedom. There were odd moments when she fell asleep in mid-sentence, but the audience always waited patiently until she awoke.

In 1861 the Civil War broke out, and Harriet discovered her next mission. The governor of Massachusetts, John Andrew, sent her to the Union Army, where she worked as a cook, nurse, scout, and spy. But she couldn't resist taking a more active part. On June 2, 1863, Tubman helped lead a raid on the Combahee River in which some 750 slaves were freed.

Tubman joined the Union Army as spy and nurse after the Civil War broke out.

Final Years

When the Civil War finally ground to a halt in 1865, the United States Congress approved the Thirteenth Amendment to the Constitution, officially freeing all slaves. For the first time in her life, Tubman was a woman without a mission.

But Harriet soon found a new one. Women were not allowed to vote at that time, and a group of women called suffragists had formed a movement to fight for this basic right. Harriet Tubman became one of the movement's most respected supporters and speakers.

Meanwhile, Tubman took care of her aging parents and helped raise money for newly freed slaves. But times were hard. Even though she was famous, money was short. In 1868 a woman named Sarah Hopkins Bradford decided to help by writing Harriet Tubman's life story. Based on many interviews, the book, *Scenes in the Life of Harriet Tubman,* was published in 1869. Tubman used the money she received from the sale of the book to pay off the mortgage on her Auburn home.

In the spring of 1869 Tubman remarried. She lived with her husband, Nelson Davis, until 1888, when he died of tuberculosis. In the meantime, both of Tubman's parents had died sometime in the 1870s. Both were close to one hundred years old.

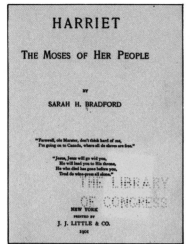

In 1886 Sarah Bradford published a second edition of her book about Harriet Tubman called *Harriet, the Moses of Her People*. Tubman used the money from this book to set up an old-age home. In 1908 she donated her home and some land to the African Methodist Episcopal Zion Church for use as a home for the sick.

Harriet Tubman lived to be a very old woman, respected throughout the country and loved in her adopted town of Auburn. Neighbors looked forward to her visits, when, over a cup of tea, she would describe her adventures on the Underground Railroad.

Harriet Tubman died peacefully on March 10, 1913. A year later, the city of Auburn honored her in a ceremony. Speeches were made, and a stone tablet was presented, which read in part:

In memory of Harriet Tubman.
Born a slave in Maryland about 1821.
Died in Auburn N.Y., March 10th 1913.
Called the Moses of her people,
during the Civil War. With rare
courage she led over three hundred
negroes up from slavery to freedom,
and rendered invaluable service as nurse and spy.

IMPORTANT DATES IN THE LIFE OF HARRIET TUBMAN

1820? Araminta Ross, known as Harriet, is born on the Brodas plantation in Maryland.

1831 Nat Turner leads his famous slave revolt.

1844 Harriet marries John Tubman.

1849 Tubman escapes slavery. She makes friends with abolitionists of the Philadelphia Vigilance Committee.

1850–52 Tubman brings many slaves north using the Underground Railroad.

1852 Tubman makes her first trip to Canada.

1858 Tubman's career as a public speaker begins in Boston.

1861–64 Tubman works as a spy and nurse for the Union Army.

1868 Sarah Hopkins Bradford publishes *Scenes in the Life of Harriet Tubman*.

1908 Tubman residence becomes a home for sick and elderly blacks.

1913 Tubman dies in Auburn, New York, on March 10.

A special stamp honoring the memory of Harriet Tubman was issued on February 1, 1978, the opening day of the first Black History Month.

FIND OUT MORE
ABOUT HARRIET TUBMAN

Books: *Freedom Train: The Story of Harriet Tubman* by Dorothy Sterling (New York: Scholastic, 1987).

Go Free or Die: A Story About Harriet Tubman by Jeri Ferris (Minneapolis, Minn.: Carolrhoda Books, 1988).

Harriet Tubman by Rae Bains (Mahwah, N.J.: Troll Associates, 1982).

Harriet Tubman by Francene Sabin (Mahwah, N.J.: Troll Associates, 1985).

Harriet Tubman by Kathie B. Smith (New York: Messner, 1989).

Harriet Tubman by Kathie B. Smith and Pamela Z. Bradbury (New York: Simon & Schuster, 1989).

Wanted Dead or Alive: The True Story of Harriet Tubman by Ann McGovern (New York: Scholastic, 1991).

Places: In Auburn, New York, are found Harriet Tubman's house and the African Methodist Episcopal Zion Church, where Harriet Tubman went on many Sundays to pray and sing.

Also in Auburn, a plaque was erected in 1932 in honor of her heroic commitment to freedom.

INDEX